Chasing Down
the
Storm

Charles R. Castle, Jr.
Poems 2017-2019

Improbable Press

Eugene, Oregon

The Princess of Babylon Beach was published in the
Oregon Poetry Association *Verseweavers* Anthology 2017

First Printing, 2019

ISBN: 9781088457542

Sandra

for

love

Erik and Paul

for

friendship

I am in my best self

when I can feel the poetry in words

I fear chiefly lest my expression

not be extra-vagant enough, may not wander

far enough beyond the narrow limits

of my daily experience, so as to be adequate

to the truth of which I am convinced

Henry David Thoreau

Table of Contents

Ω

Ω

Ω

Clouds and Clarity

In the beginning
    there was the word . . .
. . . but no punctuation

What of commas
    and semicolons if we write

to obscurity
    paraphrasing the obvious

With storms in all forms
    we weather the world

    dress appropriately

Let's Have Words

Let's have words
Small ones at first
      like shards of glass
Pull them from your skin if necessary
      from the broken windows
      of your memory
Imagine you were a church once

Were you singular and alone
      on some far hill with a
      simple steeple
Or were you a cathedral
      in the city square where
      you sheltered the poor
      and gave them faith

Do you remember the day
      when the bombs fell that shattered
      your windows and shook your faith
The day you knew the world was at war

Let's have words
Make them beautiful if you must
      in the face of war or make them

---

as ugly and twisted as the face

of an orphan crying

Bring us the child's tears when

they were your tears

Bring us the words your mother whispered

in the night when your father

went missing and you felt her fear

Let's have words

like the sun rising when you knew love

was possible and wars could end

Bring us your vocabulary of flowers

with their fragrances

Tell us where you will plant them

outside the church you are

rebuilding now

Reconstruction

I am rebuilding a war-damaged church
   mixing the mortar of loss
   with the water of promise

I do not build to pierce the sky
   but to cup a heart on its altar

These stacked bricks make walls
   to frame stained-glass windows
   while all about them reigns
   an indifferent world

At the edge of this emptiness
   I try to remember
   why I pray

We Rose out of Deep Grass

As a child along the streams of New England
As a boy on the unkept fields of school yards

As a bud on a branch of a family tree
As something green reaching for clouds

With ancestry written in the palm of our hand we rose
Out of deep grass as unsuppressed desire and flew

On wings the sky was made for into an unseen web
And by its nature filled the moments of our days

A Contrast of Birds

In Oregon, land of mountains,
  rivers and fertile valleys,
  black crows in the shimmer of rain
  turn over leaves like tarot cards.

  From their divinations
  they speak to us in our dreams.

In Maine, where I was born,
  grey gulls on beaches vexed by wind
  crack the shells of winter crabs
  like angry priests.

  Without premonition
  they recite their blind belief.

Anger

There is a sharp, broken blade
    caught side-ways in my throat.

I'd like to be subtle about it,
    having lived with it so long.

I'd like to give it a name
    like Leroy or Nadine.

But it's from a time
    before grade school
    when I didn't know the name
    for things that should not
    be swallowed.

Dante's Paradox

There is a rage in me
   set like fire upon the world.
There is a love in me
   that forgives my rage.

All my bones aflame
   become smoke and ash,
Yet some intention flares,
   and burns to be free.

Each step the angel craves
   the fallen also takes,
Hand in hand by fire and praise
   and neither holds the other back.

Critique

When they told you
>> Thou shall not kill,
>>> but war will make a man of you.
>> Everyone loves a parade.

When they told you
>> If it's in the good book it's true, now turn
>>> to the next hymn on this dismal day.
>> God has a plan for you,
>>> art isn't part of it.

When they told you
>> In couch cushions you sometimes find
>>> loose change. Beware of change.
>> Good things come to those who wait,
>>> keep waiting.
>> Life is for living, but why risk it.
>> Ignorance is bliss, be happy.
>> Clean up, janitors will always have work.
>> Someday your ship will come in,
>>> prepare to row.
>> Don't look in the mirror,
>>> failure reflects badly.
>> Peace of mind comes at a price,
>>> you can't afford it.

When they told you
>> You're part of a better tomorrow,
>>> vote for me.

Change is possible, we'll let you know
    when it happens.

When they told you
        Diamonds are forever,
            the bigger the better.
        Third time's a charm.
        Laughter is the best medicine,
            possible side effects include . . . .

When they told you
        Don't sweat the small stuff.
        State your full name.
        Sign here.
        If I were you.
        When you retire.
        In the next life.
        Better luck next time.

When they told you
        There's a right and a wrong way,
            just the way you're doing it.

When they told you
        A good word counts for everything,
            if you change these
            you might
            have a poem.

From Where I Sit

I have gone back in my mind,
    but I cannot go back to the British Isles
    of my ancestry.

All the history that chained us then,
    chains us now,
    and I cannot go back in chains.

We landed on the shores of Barnstable
    when they said we could not go back
    on pain of death.
So we brought our pain with us.

How far have we come since then
    with these chains dragging
    from the east?

We have come crossing oceans of our fears.
We have come as sailors
    and fishermen.
I have tasted their blood in my mouth.
They have offered me safe harbor.

I have known the women who farmed
   the wilderness with their hard hands.
They have cradled me and fed me
   their loneliness and apple pie.

I have seen the sun rise over the bay
   at Cape Cod, but cannot go back,
   my fears, in a scallop shell,
   are buried there.

Today, I have invited them to sit with me
   at my doorstep facing west,
   the salt wind blowing
   windchimes forged from chains.

Planted

Entering my sixty-seventh summer
    through doors of a long winter,
    high green grasses border
    spring gardens where peas
Climb trellises again.

I am fenced by these years,
    bending to turn earth as I
    am turned by it,
    both sower and seed
    surfacing from rich soil,
Greening toward light.

If You See My Brother

I would ask you if you've seen my brother.
I've been looking for him along all these roads.
I was told he'd been seen out on the margins.
I was told he was just moving through.
Our family has not seen him,
  we've had no word from him in years.
My parents died not knowing
  and in their final days forgot his name.
I still remember we looked alike,
  his features older though.
I still remember we looked alike,
  though the photos are long gone.
My sisters were too young then.
For them he's like a dream,
  yet they are looking for him also,
  each in her own way.

In his youth I was told he took odd jobs,
  got by on words and deeds.
He slept where sunsets found him
  along a river of dusty places.
He might have joined a union once,
  mining coal or in the Merchant Marine,
  or packin' alongside migrants,

pickin' in the San Juaquin.
Someone said they saw him in Alberta
   during Vietnam.
He might have had a family once.
He might have been fishin' salmon in the 70's
   out of Aberdeen.
He's been gone so long now, but I still have hope
   he'll show up or our paths will cross.
I keep my eyes peeled, maybe you will too.
I'd like to look in his eyes before the chance is lost.

In the 80's some say he drove freight
   down the 5 into Mexico.
Some say he was doing 10 for runnin' weed,
   I just don't know.
He took risks, but he didn't gamble much.
I heard that in a truck stop outside of Vegas once.
I've checked records.
I've checked the forwarding address.
I've seen rental checks stamped insufficient funds.
On a construction site in Barstow
   I saw a toolbelt and worn out boots
   a foreman said my brother loaned to a new guy
   who worked a week and he had to fire.

My last near miss was back in '99.

A cop in Needles said he was busted up

in an accident on the Interstate.

Maybe he was using another name

in a car with Montana plates.

He must have been fifty when he broke both legs.

The hospital never did get paid.

In a strip club in Baton Rouge, a dancer said

she'd lived with him for a year or more,

but they broke up after Katrina hit.

Where he went from there no one knows for sure.

I keep hearin' news from places east and west.

He walks with a limp these days,

he's getting' by.

They look at me and say the likeness is striking.

Who knows what's true after all these years.

I just know I missed him growing up.

I'm still lookin' for the brother I didn't have

out on the margins along all these roads.

If you see him, tell him,

it's not too late to come home.

Cremation

The nurse pulled the sheet over my father's face.
Someone from the morgue, six floors below,
   rode a service elevator like a boat crossing a river.
I could imagine the ride down,
   having worked in that hospital for years,
   having ridden with a few corpses at various times
   in the silence the dead bring.
I could remember the half-lit basement,
   quiet as stone at two am.
I knew the dark hallway with its double doors.

I wasn't surprised to watch him rolled away,
   slipped noiselessly on rubber wheels,
   into the fluorescent pool of elevator light
   on his wood-paneled journey out of this world.
It was the morning of the sixth day.
The extended family had departed the evening before
   knowing this morning would come.

I suppose you could say I felt
   at peace with my father's death,
   having spent those days in that room, when
   at eleven pm, he took his last breath.

And I suppose you could say I'd begun grieving
  months before as he became frailer at ninety.
Maybe it was November when we sat
  in the funeral home, nicely appointed, respectfully
  quiet, when we made the final arrangements,
  and wrote the check.

But on the night he released his final breath,
  in the stillness that remained after,
  and with that total stillness in his face,
  it was then I thought, how strange to be rolled
  into shadows through double doors.

And I was left to wonder, as I do now five years later,
  what part of letting go, like smoke on the wind,
  are we missing when we are not present
  while the body burns?

Twist-tied Ghost

In this south-hills nursing home
    ghosts and their familiars walk the long hall
    between the beginning and the end.
We watch them struggle on their journey
    as they pass my mother's open door.
Out her winter window I see in mist,
    beneath a broken awning's crush,
    the CNAs smoke cigarettes and exhale
    apparitions I watch drift away.
The tired nurses make their morning rounds
    to keep a restless peace as best they can.
Here, there are as many ways to die
    as there are stars, and since my father's death
    a month before, my mother knows how long
    a night can be. She knows how far the fall is
    to the floor and waits the way her stars reveal.

We waited when my father fell
    and suddenly was gone
        in five short days
        in a hospital bed
        in a morphine sleep
        in a room with a view
        on a night in July
        with a pension check in the mail.

My mother's view is not green hills and sunrise,
  but an asphalt alley by evening.
I stare into it knowing faces aren't transparent
  and no one can tell the living from the dead.
In the fading light at my mother's table,
  I sign my father's checks,
  I pay my mother's bills.
I count the days he's been gone by the multiples
  of hours my mother knows.
There are peaceful deaths and labored deaths,
  with no way to know which will come for you.

I leave by the backdoor through the alley
  to find my car under streetlight and heavy rain.
I drive the distance down a narrow night,
  drifting through reflecting streets.

The mortuary closes at six. I do not hurry.
In a plastic bag,
        in a cardboard box
        in the undertaker's office
        my father's ashes are twist-tied
        like craft-store clay
        bulk food
        or fertilizer.

When the Apples Were Ripening

Father, when the apples were ripening
   I waited for you.
It was summer and the undertaker's daughter
   had just left with the circus.
I wanted to ask you, on that evening
   watching her flagged caravan depart,
   how what I thought was love could die.

Father, I remember when you were a tree—
   all your years bearing fruit, standing with you
   on the banks of the Mad River.
We were fishermen then.

I remember you taught me there is a depth
   to things like rivers, like trees.

You said
But love is the most mysterious
   of all deep things.

You said

Son, fish there

   along the faster currents. Learn to read

   how the water moves. Become a fish

   in your heart and when you become hungry

   let someone catch you,

   because . . .

      that's how love works.

And when you are caught by love,

   tend to the years you are given

   like trees

   until you are an orchard.

Don't ask for anything

   from the undertaker's daughter.

   She's been where she's going.

Go where you have not been, my son.

Mystery will find you there. It is she

   who will love you deeply,

   and that is sweet,

   sweet fruit, indeed.

Day at the Beach

Death
    We will inject it
    with just enough beauty
    to make it tolerable.

Pain
    We will call it death.
    Tell the poor man
    it was inevitable.

Love
    We will call it pain.
    Tell our children
    it was the best we could do.

Our children
    will call it a day at the beach
    when the tide
    comes in like death.

Ω

Succulent Heart

Love weaves a web

She takes her throne

Ask how many spiders

Sit down beside her

In Love and Desire

In the details
of her beauty,
stature and glow,
he saw gods
dancing with devils

and could not
look away.

~

In love and desire,
in lust and madness,
are the small lies
we tell ourselves
resisting

the urge
to speak the truth.

Unspeakable Beauty

Still wet from swimming,
Exposed in full sun ten feet away,
Her towel and suit hanging in hand,
Ocean beach in the distance,
The arcade pier, the outdoor café,
The day just begun,
My table in the shade at the street crossing,
The rising steam of my coffee,
My notebook, my desire in my pen.

The way light seemed to ripple around her,
    off the sparse down of blond hair on her skin,
Her butterscotch thighs,
The back of her knees,
The "just so" bend to her wrist when
    she brushed back her hair.
The arch in her sandaled foot,
    heel raised, red painted toes to the ground,
The sweep of her athletic back,
The shift of her hip and cling of short skirt,
The white, shear summer fabric,
Low belly exposed,
The sun creating a silhouette
    between her legs,
The shadow of the delta,

The hollow at her throat
The swell of her breast, and
　　bud of raised nipple,
The tilt of her head, eyes hidden
　　behind shades,
Her face smooth as a silk bowl,
Her unguarded innocence proud
　　as the headlands at dawn.

The way she stood against the sun and the sea
　　with the soft morning still waking in me,
How I watched her cross and walk down the street,
　　and I tried to remember how to breathe.

And how the moment was shattered
　　like a gunshot at a wedding
　　by the loud, crude howl of man passing
　　in a black pickup truck.
And I watched how she folded like a bird
　　hit by a stone.

And though I did not throw the stone,
　　I was left convicted in body and heart,
　　found guilty and sentenced.
And I looked down into the dark cell
　　of my empty cup.

Tumbler of Stones

Come my lover
>   down to the shoreline
>   the tide is high

We will gather round stones
>   rolled up the beach
>   by the sea

We will move to the waves
>   wishing we could wear
>   our imperfect love
>   smooth

Missing You

The dogwood is pink again

a year gone

like yesterday

Regret like petals falling

Hard to Say

How silly to think an erection
could save the world
   or a love affair
   or a marriage
   or avoid a bad divorce

Except on a morning
   when a bed
   went cold and unshared
   when we'd wished
   we'd said

love doesn't need
to be so hard

How I Hold You

I hold you
   like six origami cranes,
   folded and framed.

Like calligraphy,
   a Buddhist quote
   on impermanence.

Like a single line of poetry,
   imperfect in memory,
   still beautiful.

Light of Hours

I have seen her in the light of every hour,
    each a shade of the girl she wears
    like a memory from childhood.
I think I know her from another place
    when she steps wet from bathing
    and I see beneath her skin,
    her timeless child.

Yet it's through her eyes
    she shows me beauty that knows no age,
    and by the lines about them
    point to wisdom and everything
    the years have cost her.
In that gaze, so like remembering a dream,
    I hold my breath when she draws me close
    to a softer world than I have known.

And with a kiss she says to me
        Surely you remember
            this touch,
            this light,
            and all these hours of the day.

Thread of Words

If I told you how I love you
　along a thread of words,
Could you hear them as I intend,
　neither vague nor distant,
　but within your heart?

Could you feel their message—
　a glow of violet emotion
　infused in molten glass,
Or as bold desire, blood-red
　as the tulip ready to unfold?

If I hid their secret in a whisper
　and placed it behind your ear,
　would you let its shiver move you?

Or if I made them transparent,
　wrapped in ribbon
　in your drawer of silks,
Would you wear them for me knowing
　what they would reveal?

And if I painted our sheets with them
　as tall feathered cranes

Would you spread your heartfelt wings

   and let me join your dance

   and so lift our way into the sky?

If I told you how I loved you

   along a thread of words,

   would that be a love

You would understand?

Divine Therapy

Oh, but how she loves me
    by appointment twice a week.
On the couch we speak of things
    like fruit we cannot reach.
But she always keeps her hat on
    though she's naked to her bones,
She arranges them so candidly,
    I seldom feel alone.
I could say that I don't need her,
    I'm easy to deceive.
If I confess to loving her,
    I atone each time she leaves.

She Comes Like Candles

My lover
   comes like candles
   on the snows
   of Christmas Eves.
She delivers lambs and lions
   from the mangers of her sleeves.
And when she lies down with them
   the whole world is at peace,
   where I'm given my redemption
   in the light of her release.

Black-lacquered Bowl

Black-lacquered bowl reflects the light:
The chestnut porch the craftsman made,
The window where the curtains drift,
The garden and the bamboo gate.

The cherry tree on spring's return
Drops blossoms in the late day's blush.
Two doves call the evening hour
And breezes seem to hesitate.

A couple walks the garden path,
Evening's hush rests on their hearts.
In shared regard they need not talk
Where shaded maples deepen red.

Love keeps couples close as one
While night passes into dawn.
What dream can linger into day
To embrace them in their bed?

Black-lacquered bowl with water filled
Floats a lotus briefly there.
Dewed among these splendored things,
All contained and nothing said.

A Love Like Myth

Days spent climbing
with Sisyphus
fearing the grace of eagles.

Nights descending
for Euridice,
killing snakes in my dreams.

If It Doesn't Change

We'll live by bombs

And bible psalms

Do yoga until noon

Spend evening hours

At baby showers

On the dark side of the moon

Waiting for the Wine

When the world ends
by climate change or cataclysm,

    on that morning I'll wake
    to find we're out of coffee after
    our weekend at the cabin
    on the coast.
I'll be late for work and you'll be
    leaving for Spain
    with the book you're writing.
You will still have to pack
    and we might not be talking.

When the world ends
by carcinoma or fall,

    driving to the airport,
    the traffic will be terrible.
In Barcelona you'll discover
    you didn't pack your pills
    or remember to call your brother.
I'll keep the dentist waiting.
While you're away the cat will stop

using the litter box and things
will really go downhill.

When the world ends
by flood or famine,

    refrigerated food will pass its *sell-by* date,
    shopping malls may not open at ten,
    and cellphone coverage will be spotty.
We will have renewed our wine memberships,
    but club boxes will sit in warehouses
    or in trucks stuck in traffic.
Our unread books will accrue late fees,
    and it will be several weeks
    since we made love.

When the world ends
by stroke or heart attack,

    it will be four years since the kids
    moved away and two since the last time
    we visited.
But the cars will be paid for and the house,

with a new roof, will have our street
   number painted on the curb
   in our alma mater's colors.

Sitting alone, I'll binge-watch a Netflix
   second season and will have changed
   the batteries in the remote.
In your room, overlooking the ocean,
   the television won't be working
   and you might think of me.

When the world ends
by nuclear war or pandemic disease,

   if it's fall, leaves in the yard
   may be raked into piles
   and sit there for weeks.
I'll watch football in front of the big screen
   and be asleep by half-time.
You will still not have called
   and I will not have cleaned the carpets.
But anticipating your return,
   the bed will have fresh sheets
   and the wine will be chilled.

When the world ends,
by old age, as it must,

    symphony tickets will wait in will-call,
    and the airline may have lost your luggage.
There will be things we need to say
    and our dinner reservations may change.

When the world ends
and we're out of time,

    high tide will touch the beach again
    at the cabin on the coast.
Your book will not be finished, but Paris
    will look as good as Venice or Rome
    for the trip we'll plan next year.
Driving to the airport on that morning
    the traffic will be lighter
    and everything we love
    will be waiting for us
    when we return.

Category 5 Lullaby

Sleep my child the sky's not falling
The summer hills are not in flames
All your fathers are now buried
You alone must hold the blame

Sleep my child the poles aren't melting
The oceans of the world won't rise
All your brothers guard the borders
To no avail against the tide

Sleep my child there's no help coming
Our future now will be as seed
Cast at random into caverns
The wealthy few will be received

Sleep my child the ground's not shaking
It's not the sound of hurricanes
It's not the sound of nature's message
You will not build your house again

Sleep my child you've been abandoned
The halls of justice are facades
All their words serve absent masters
The dream you've bought is a mirage

Sleep my child the high ground's calling
At the edge of drought and flood
Sow your seed this devil's bargain
Is cracked in clay or drowned in mud

Sleep my child for now I leave you
Take what comfort you can find
By will not wisdom I've deceived you
Mammon's gods are deaf and blind

Down on the Streets in Boston

Rosa's homeless alleys led into winter
   where her nerves, on the icy edge
   of a breakdown, met flurries of snow
   with tears.
On the worst days they came upwelling
   like mad birds—killdeer in a gale.
It was a dire December.
She had nowhere to go.

Heaven help her, home was impossible.
She had a family history of Christmases
   where they'd buried the baby Jesus.
Her mother was as abusive to her
   as the words between them—wasps and adders.
   Oh, by the will of God, Mother's repeated refrain
   you'd be better off dead.

Rosa slept catch-as-catch-can and the men
   left her alone—she could spit bile.
Her only friends were:
   a Mass General psych nurse with a bi-polar sister,
   a man at the mission, six months sober,
   sharing a black-coffee breakfast,
   and the part-time bus driver, every other Sunday

St. Mathew's Church of the Divine
Free Lunch and Bingo.

It wasn't a friendly city.
From St. Mathew's she walked down
 where she could see the Charles River
 icing up for the holidays.
It was a thin ice, twelve days before Christmas.
It would crack like a church bell.

Looking out across the endless traffic,
 across the endless streets,
 she anticipated crossing.

The Princess of Babylon Beach

She was a princess from Long Island out on Babylon Beach.
Her daddy played the market, Momma liked to preach.
They'd fill martini glasses in the afternoons
And fight like wolves in winter under harvest moons.

Sue could have been a member in the DAR,
But she burned up her credentials in a Jersey bar.
She grew up in the sixties in an all-girls school,
Tried to measure up for Daddy with her mother's rules.

She took a tab of acid on a starry night.
It turned on all her switches and she liked the sights.
She broke a leg in theatre for a little while,
But had a thing for cocaine 'til she couldn't smile.

She walked a plank Off Broadway to a Greenwich flat
And ended up in Harlem with an alley cat.
She went to see her parents when she couldn't feel.
They said *You look like hell.* She said *No big deal.*

When she saw them in November they agreed to pay
If she'd go and get her master's and change her way.
But she was busted before Christmas for a DUI
And spent New Year's back in Harlem on a black tar high.

She pulled herself together, no one knows quite when,
Sending postcards back from Bombay in magenta pen.
Now she lives on Orcas Island in the Puget Sound
Writing books about the spirit out on holy ground.

She's got a chain of lovers spread across the world.
Inside she's wearin' a tiara, she's still daddy's girl.

Tequila up the Trapline

Tequila up the trapline
I'm singin' Patsy Cline
It's one hell of a snowstorm
Montana '89
Tequila up the trapline
I'm drivin' fast and blind
It's colder than my Polson wife
Weighin' down my mind

Five miles north of Hungry Horse
No traffic, rough terrain
I'm busted up and bleedin'
I'm not feelin' any pain
Packers Roost is 'round the bend
The lights from here look warm
Tonight the trapline's buried
In November's first big storm

I don't want beer or whiskey
But I'll buy the bar a round
It's weather meltin' in my eyes
Just set that bottle down
The snow blows deep, it's ten below
The upper road ain't clear

My truck is totaled in a ditch
My wife's down south of here

She's shacked up flush in Bigfork
With a Bozeman friend of mine
She won't be home 'til Tuesday
I'm stuck here for a time
We'd make love on nights like this
On the floor before our fires
Now it's autumn wood I stack alone
When she leaves with her desires

Ain't seen our kid for fifteen years
She's livin' in LA
We raised her here 'til high school
She turned thirty yesterday
There's nothin' left but ashes
The homestead burned last spring
I was drinkin' to *The Thrill is Gone*
In a bar with BB King

Take this ten for quarters
Your jukebox looks brand new

Patsy Cline's my date tonight

And she's way overdue

My heart's back in that totaled truck

I'm gonna be just fine

I'll dance real slow with Patsy

So don't pay me any mind

Tequila up the trapline

I'm singin' Patsy Cline

It's one hell of a snowstorm

Montana '89

Tequila up the trapline

I'm drivin' fast and blind

It's colder than my Polson wife

Weighin' down my mind

If tequila was a snowplow

And a shotgun was a glass

I'd take this bottle to my truck

And see how long I'd last

I'm torn up in a snowstorm

On the far end of the line

Patsy let's go dancin'

There's still a little time

When the Truth Hurts

Load the gun son

We're going to shoot the messenger

He's hunting quail up on the Bixbee Road

Accidents happen all the time

    and his turn's overdue

Load the gun son

I never liked what he had to say

Ω

American Facade

How long can a mask endure
And overlook a dream derailed
To preach a gospel so impure
With negligence so thinly veiled

The Generation That Followed

In the generation that followed the generation that followed
many were with the years as they had always been no more
and no less as if they had been born to them again and again
finding themselves there without question as if on a hill
where they were taught to admire the holes in their hands
and feet and to expect there would be nails for everyone
needing ladders to build towers where they would all make
the great sacrifice in the generation that followed

Once it had been in their nature to be green and it was in
them naturally as if they had been born to it again and again
out of green dust and water where women went around
picking green things they had been taught to pick over and
over until they were picked and they made babies and some
were girls and some were boys and life came into life until
they made gods because they thought children needed them
and they forgot in the generation that followed to pick green
things

In the generation that followed the generation that followed
they loved no less than they loved and they hated no less than
this where in their faith they feared and in their fear they
prospered and livelihood became business and fear became
good for business so they taught their children to fear more
for they had learned to fear well though it made them sick

In the generation that followed they followed the God they created and made great strides saying *God is Great Everywhere* but many were not everywhere they were only where they were so they made God great there and the god elsewhere became less great in the generation that followed

In the generation that followed they learned to love their great God over all others including each other and they learned to fear the other's god and so hated them greatly in the generation that followed where in the name of their God they created great wars and though war was not good either for children or green living things it was good for business and while they feared war they learned to live with it though many died

In the generation that followed the many wars made them industrious and there was steady work in great factories making bullets that were like nails and there were enough of them for everyone to make holes in their hands and feet and they made many sacrifices to the God they had learned to love and hate more than the love that was in their nature

Until at last in the generation that followed the generation that followed they made the greatest sacrifice having nowhere green to go nor a single star to guide them as they wandered the rusted rusted land

Who's the Boss of Star Wars

Conversation between Noah 7 and Eli 5 at lunch.

N: God made everything.

E: Not houses or babies.

N: God made Jesus when he was a baby. But Jesus is God.

E: Jesus is God?

N: Yes, and Jesus is God's kid.

E: What?! Okay, well, who's the boss of Star Wars?

She Felt the New Migration

One day
    she woke up and said

> *All the fish have turned over*
> *in the sea.*
> *They migrate to a new gravity.*

And sure enough,
    when the fishermen
    cast their great nets
    the nets rose like hot-air balloons
    in a sky filled with bones
        that flapped their tails.

All the While Hollyhocks

All the while hollyhocks
Grow among the poppies
Their stems above the garden
Through the politics of summer

By perspective it's transparent
We do not rise above it
Self-interest is the gospel
That perpetuates the land

Complacent and complicit
Lulled by comfort's indecision
We can barely float an interest
On our tide of disregard

When power and its influence
Control the conversation
We sink beneath the shadow
The future holds in store

All the while hollyhocks
Grow among the poppies
Their stems above the garden
Through the politics of summer

And if they bloom in August
They will seed another season
The purple of their flowers
All the news that we can bear

How we've little expectation
The elections in November
Will usher in a springtime
For the challenges at hand

Where another generation
Wants for peace and promise
And hopes the world tomorrow
Will be ruled by equal justice

All the while hollyhocks
Grow among the poppies
Their stems above the garden
Through the politics of summer

Crown of Creation

This is how we crown ourselves
On evolution's tree
As sovereign gods that rule the world
With nature at our knees

We prune away the branches
From the Tree of Life
Where we steward each extinction
With a dogma as our knife

Convinced of our salvation
In some heaven in the skies
Life itself is threatened
By the nature of these lies

Sooner would the ants sing hymns
Or blackbirds crucify their best
Than all the kingdoms bow their heads
That man alone be blessed

4th of July

He said *Let us go down like roosters*
Under the flag and fireworks
And crow a little

I said *No, let us go down*
To the broken city
Blind as Cro Magnon men

He said *Let's wear funny hats*
Made from stars and stripes
March in a parade

I said *Let's fight apartheid in*
Poughkeepsie, the KKK in Kalamazoo
Let's die trying

He said *Where's your patriotism*
Your white pride and
Your privilege

I said *On a common at Kent State*
Under a river in El Salvador
Buried in Arlington with those who died
To make a dream come true

When They Send the Trucks

We will escape by the backdoor of night.
We will take old forest roads, the ones
   the loggers drove when trees were green,
   before the endless fires
   of these smoke-filled skies.

We will escape by the backdoor of night,
   when we're alerted they've reached the bridge
   where our children, on rope swings swung,
   before the water was diverted
   to cool the great machine.

We will escape by the backdoor of night.
We will watch dust rise on switchbacks
   as trucks ascend and we hold each other
   as we did when we were free
   before the coup.

We will escape by the backdoor of night,
   having watched our last sunrise,
   having spoken our love for each other,
   having read our final poems, the way we did
   before they were crimes.

We will escape by the backdoor of night
    when the first gunshots of resistance are heard,
    but before missiles hit the meadows,
    when we climb to ridgelines waving our flags
    and we flee into ice caves
    and yesterday's better dreams.

Leaving Latin America

On a Salvadorian beach a young girl
  watched a woven bag of memories
  be swallowed by the tide.
The wind erased her hollow steps in the sand.

Out on a high desert
  a car burned in the night.
Hard rain fell, drowning footprints.

At dawn a wet progression slipped
  down narrow streets into a dangerous city.
They carried grandmother's bean pupusas
  and her tearful blessings.
They slept beneath volcanoes in the church plaza
  and waited for the sun.

The days were long.
Seen from afar a thin line walked north
  in a wavering heat.
Days became weeks
  and the weeks wore on them.
For two thousand miles candles
  burned on temporary altars, prayers
  to an exodus of spirit.

There were flags at every border,

    soldiers at every crossing,

    there were good reasons to move on.

When the fathers walked,

    they walked with children in their arms.

When the mothers rested,

    they rested with children on their knees.

They crossed themselves at the desperate river

    when the babies cried.

Further north, under the stars

    and stripes, American border guards

    behind razor-wire fences

    drove tent stakes

    into the heart of the land.

Ω

Under a Green-Leafed Sky

Under a green-leafed sky
Our branched lives grow.
We count the days of June
As if they could not end.
We sleep our morning slumbers
Rich as momentary thieves.
We walk, in bliss, these fields,
These flowered gardens.
In such grace as this we rest
Our summer souls in peace.

Oregon

Cool as the breeze off Mount Hood's shoulders.

Regal as Multnomah's Falls.

Beacon bright off Astoria headlands.

Silver and gold, Columbia your crown.

Come John Day in your morning colors,

Sun warm from the serpentine east border.

Deschutes through your stone spillways.

Santiam and Sandy clear in your promise.

Cascade Sahalie, sing loud from your heart.

Take away breath from the cloud-capped peaks

Old volcanoes on your spine.

Your vistas in all directions weaving wonder,

McKenzie and Klamath treasures,

Umpqua to Ashland and the gold country dream,

South into the mystery of caves.

All your rare and hidden destinations,

Out of mountain passes, valleys and canyons,

High plains and estuaries, beyond

Flooded embankments and dry summer stream beds.

Cradle us in the majesty of your Crater Lake.

Run wild forever and deep, the Rogue, by all of us.

Rest us on your dunes.

Raise us on your promontory beauty.

Stand us in awe before the ocean.

The love we have for you

Leans us westward

Always seeking more.

Hiking Sweet Creek

Carved in the west slope of the Coast Range,
Sweet Creek enters the Siuslaw River
Ten miles downstream from Mapleton.

A narrow road competes for space
Where the creek flows between foothills,
Through what is less a valley,
Than a series of hollows
Of pastureland and small farms.

Not far above the green lowlands
Sweet Creek flows freely over bedrock.
Where, at the lower trailhead,
It begins to fill pools carved by waterfalls.
Soon a hard-won trail hugs the wall
Of an intimate canyon. Which, ferned
And flowered in spring, progresses gradually
Under a dense moss-covered tower of cedar and fir.
A few, toppled by storm with huge root balls upturned,
Show fresh gravel scars washed out by rain.

The scene is natural and wild,
Yet not intimidating. It is a sanctuary

Of water song, visual in small portraits,
Revealed slowly over two miles
Up a gentle ascent.

Notable is the steel and iron work
At Annice Falls— a narrow walkway
With its i-beam supports, its heavy grating,
Its large anchor bolts drilled in stone.

What this work affords
Is easy access to the upper falls
For families with infant children,
All manner of dogs on leashes,
Older couples with their limitations,
And young lovers, all of them ascending
In ease and anticipation.
And in time, returning in gratitude.

They return where they began, changed perhaps,
With a sense of sharing a hidden place.
A place with a history.
Perhaps knowing the names on two plaques,
Or at least carrying

The memory of Sweet Creek's

Sound and color as a discovery

Of another piece of Oregon's graciousness

Many have loved and many

Have worked to protect.

Geysers

Geysers of black bats rise
from the chimneys of caves
silhouettes
against diminishing blue

Evening's insects
like the stars
devoured by morning

Windchime Cat

Look how the windchimes call
the cat to nap

and all my pages curl
toward evening

plum wine
in the poet's cup
may make him dance where love
sometimes walks
but it's only with his muse
he takes the chance
and talks

There Are No Words

There are no words
not set in stone
that can't be changed

erased

or by another
order placed
upon the page

arranged

in multiples
of combinations   by
a simple fascination

tried

imagination
in the moment open
to some distant

almost

perfect
destination

In the Great Room

The world is hard enough, my friend,
Steel-barred and iron-crossed.
Beneath our solitary cells weave tunnels.

Just beyond the border wall,
A desert storm as vast as time.
Throw caution to the wind.

Ride a camel on a silver thread.
Hold the needle very still.
Through it into Eden.

Pass a rage of wolves.
White doves on an olive branch.
Sealed caves in a mountain cliff.

Below, the city, horizon to horizon.
Sounds of golden horns,
Street-corner oracles.

Go down at midnight.
Nymphs and orphans
Bathing in fountains.

Call softly the muse's name,
Sit elixir-ed on caballine streets.
By dawn slip into the great room.

Look up at its painted sky,
Garden beneath heaven.
Climb by ladder or rise by wing

And with an artist's brush
Lift, by imperceptible measure,
The lazy finger
On the outstretched hand above.

A Place for a Poem to Live

When you create a place for a poem to live,
Lower the ceiling and dim the lights.
Round the corners with opaque shadows
Where spectral visitation may take form.

When you create a place for a poem to live,
Beg a seat for strangers, welcome them in.
Hold a space in the hollow of your chest
For the friend who will not come again.

When you create a place for a poem to live,
Misalign the chairs, scatter cushions.
Open a place at the bar, infuse the wine
With laughter, and toast the poet's tears.

Mingle people close, shoulder and thigh.
Let their cares and differences fall away.
Let the air be moved by unseen forces,
Emanations demanding voice.

Let time bend before the gravity of a podium,
Its small light brave against the darkness,
Its familiar fire, ancient and communal,
Bright in the silence before the word.

Let it usher an arrival from a distance
Spoken to life in the parsing of a line,
In the turning of a page—cryptic or lyric,
Oracle or nature born.

When you create a place for a poem to live,
Let inspiration summon apparitions, incarnations
Like Cheshire cats. No one knows on nights like this
On whose shoulders they might appear.

Beauty's Lips of Fog

Paint our sails as portraits
florid or sparsely hung

Redolent arks as emotions
plundered to couplets

The sea's face neither
candid nor callous

Its sun-rusted eyes
two wooden ships

Deserted on oceans
burning beneath azure

~

Paint the solemn wreck
a palette of grey

Beauty in mourning
not a tear in any line

The facade of her stern

silent as one raised fist

Charred mast a finger
held to her lips of fog

Along the beach she walks
splinters of truth for feet

Sprouts

April's peas push through loam
Sun finds breaks in clouds
I wait for sweet green pods
Reading poems of Po Chü-i
   a trellis for my thoughts

Ω

Mystery's Angels

Invited to dance
on the head of a pin
all my angels
masked for Mardi Gras

decline

Ashes of the Father

In the blue-hour morning,
   dark as dogs and wolves,
   there's neither silence
   nor poems.

Out in the streets,
   mad men rumble
   like trains.
I hear them.

How they echo
   down alleys
   in their fires and furies,
Shouting to God.

On careless nights
   I would join them
   setting myself aflame,
One last time.

All my sleeping children
   would hear my prayer
   in a manic language
And be restless in their dreams.

They would hear my towered wind
   tearing at powerlines
   yet leaving cats on porches
Quiet and content.

Out of the pockets of my love
   I'd place trinkets from their childhoods,
   cryptic keys, and devotions
On their doorsteps.

I would paint in neon on their streets:
   Unlock your box of memories
   Ignite and run like trains
   Scatter your father's ashes
   Join me where poems are made.

What We Leave Behind

A radical seed,
a body sprouting in a sift
  of star dust.

An affirmation
not made of summer wheat,
  neither locust,
  nor buried mole.

Even if our heads
are stuffed with straw,
  we are not hollow here.
We simply have not set
  our fields on fire.

We work a leavened sky
  with wooden tools
  while our hearts wait
  harvest under the sun.

And we would burn the world
  to see by such a light,
  to not run blindly where our lives
  are leading us.

For we are carried on a mystery of wind,

  next year's seed,

  last year's ash.

We reach to hold what can't be held,

leaving to life those we have given life,

and leaving behind us

  lines of scattered words

    in uneven rows.

It Ain't Love Honey

Don't ask me what it is
But it ain't love

Keep your company
Comfort and compromise
It ain't love
It's a slow immolation
A rehearsal for avoidance
A practiced pretending
A sleeping safe distance
It's a trapped passing of time
But it ain't love

Not freedom
Not discovery
More like a concealment
A circular repetition
A vacuum of habit

Laws are meant to be broken
What's a sofa have to offer
Set the alarm
Keep your council
Count your blessings

Break a leg

Pack a bag

Take a journey

Don't blame the lame

We got one more day

Let's wake up early

Nobody cares what we do

You want love

Let's get out and make it

There ain't no one here

Gonna bring it to you

Plant Me Deep

You think I am the seed of a man,
I am ribs and arms in a shirt you bought
   to match your clothes.
I am a halved-other, a cutout.
I walk between you and city traffic,
   between you and your cling of fears.
I hollow a pillow of flowers
   on your bed of paths and gates.
But I am contrary bones
   born of the dust of things.
I walk in bellicose boots left outside
   unlocked doors. I dance,
   all these nights unnoticed, in pooled light
   on your half-dreamt streets.
You wonder why you cannot sleep.

I am an errant seed blown over a fence.
I have flown in the belly of a bird,
   been dropped on stone, left unopened
   for a hundred years.
The morning you find me in your garden
   I am unrooted.
What kind of love stems a man green?
Drop me on your lips, plant me deep.
I am a bone-trellis for something raised
   out of the dry earth.

When I Thought the Dark

When I thought the dark
  had become blackbird eyes
  I closed mine
  and went looking for you.

It did not go well.

Numb as a morning toad
  I bumped my way toward you,
  crying my croaked refrain.
    Why am I blind.
    Where has my small
       light gone.

All around me the blackbirds sang
    charity   charity

Having given me everything,
  you gave me the darkness too.

The Weight

He would go down to the ocean at night
    with two wool blankets and a pillow.
He'd sleep hidden in the undulating dunes
    hoping the earth would shake
    somewhere he couldn't feel.
And sometime in the night the ocean
    would grow silent as it receded
    and he would sleep so deeply under the stars
    he could not hear the great wave come.

The Spider Where I Work

In the cold warehouse
where I work
there's a spider
in the bathroom.

There's a black spider
in the corner at the floor.
I've seen the egg sacks hatch
into a thousand pinpoints
sharing her color.

The web she weaves
is the size of my hand.
It runs to a small tunnel
the width of my little finger.
It disappears into a dark place
beneath ragged sheetrock.

The black spider hangs upside
down for hours an inch
off the ground.
She never sees the sun.

If frightened she will hide,

but not for long.

She's been there for months.
She's been there all my life.
She's always been there.

Last Rites for an Old Religion

With the land in drought, blackbirds bide their time.
In a cornfield one hundred monkeys, seated in a circle,
   convene as scribes.
Philosophers, stuffed with straw, hang on posts—
   scarecrows miming the wisdom of the ages.

The birds, in feathered vestments woven
   by old gods, inspire
   the monkeys to write,
         In the beginning there was the word,
         and with the word, the end . . .

The earth rumbles across the landscape,
   and though there is no wind,
   acres of dry stalks shake and gather.

Birds speak and monkeys write,
         . . . what this way comes.

Under a bitter moon, blackbirds pray
   a litany of dark indulgences.
Out of thorny hedgerows timid rabbits chorus
   the maledictions.

The composition continues,

> *It was neither the best, nor worst of times,*
> *but would be soon.*

Under frayed tassels, black rats
  gnaw corncobs at the knees of scarecrows.
  The sound alone inspires,

> *A pocket full of posies,*
> *ashes, ashes. All fall down.*

Monkeys, rabbits and rats
  bow their heads.
Birds cross themselves with a final,

> *Amen.*

And so, it was written,

> *And so, it will be.*

Border of the New Wilderness

We will meet in the meadow,
Arrive as your shadow,
Let your face be a mask.

We will meet after midnight
With forged sets of papers—
Our titles and degrees.

We will suffer common madness
With the enemy we've created
Hidden deep within us.

We will crawl through gaps in memory,
Barbed fences of our dignity,
Tearing the skin of our entitlements.

We will battle silent demons
With compassion as our weapon
And forgive them into messengers of faith.

We will fight our misconceptions
On the plains of meditation
In a quiet revolution.

We will bind our wounds each morning

And face the days before us

To create a lasting peace.

We will guard the mindful border

So no fear can return us

As slaves to fields and factories

With shadows as our masters.

We Shall Name Him 'Bitter Blaze'

Amargo on fire,
   his mind racing, slipping
   through a rope of alleys, limping in song
   past shadows. We call after him – *Amargo.*
We whisper our endearment, yet
   this love is useless. He can't hear us.

Amargo swift as flames, love
   is not what he chases. It's the source
   of love he seeks beyond his fingertips.
Look how he reaches, thin arms extended,
   where he sees the parted veil,
   the shimmered air, the bleeding light,
   where haloed crows, dark and beautiful, hover
   as a pledge of angels.
They share their close-held songs
   as love not born from man, but from the blood
   of suns, and he, with flooded eyes,
   is speared through all his separateness
   into a wailing joy.

Amargo's heart stampedes, wild
   on molten haunches. It towers without
   fear, without misgiving.

His burning visions drive him, push him

   past our open doors. No tears stalk him.

Our concerned glances go unnoticed. He runs,

   he runs, he runs through his street of days.

In the spent nights, alone and careless,

   Amargo sleeps in abandoned factories where

   dreams were forged. He lies restless and hums

   against rusted machines.

When we call to him, across our shared darkness,

   he cannot hear us. His ears attend

   to the rarest voices of long-lost stars.

We are echoes to him when we ask,

   Amargo on fire, when will you wake

   and sing to us the conflagration of your heart?

Inspired by F.G. Lorca's Amargo footnote - *In Search of Duende*

Passing Through

I am trying to find a place to lie down,
  a small place with shade
  that would welcome me.
It need not be green with spring leaves,
  nor have a view to the sea,
Just a gentle slope north toward the horizon
  to be a pillow for my head.

I am trying to find one perfect, smooth stone,
  still wet with morning dew,
  not to have it dry in my hand,
  but to sit beside it as the sun rises
  and tell my story.

I am trying to find the words to describe
  how a stone would feel light,
  and what light would feel passing through stone,
  a memory I have from before I was born.
You might remember it too.

I am trying to find in the lines on my palm,
  how I have traversed these crossings,
  each divergence separating me,
  and returning me here.

What passes for permanence along these byways,
    but desire and dream?
Here, where the wind kicks up
    all my reasons for leaving.
Have you passed this way as well?

I am trying to find, not in a kiss, nor an embrace,
    nor in a child's arms around my neck,
    but in the unexpected expression in your eyes,
    what you would tell me
    if we had words for such things,
How time has come to rest on you,
    and if you have taken any comfort from it.

I am trying to find, by laying my body down,
    the place a hand rests on a beating heart
    making it still as a wet stone.
And there become absent in the disappearing dew
    waiting to join with you
    in the sun's wind
    making the northern sky glow again.

Taken in Passing

Chess pieces don't tell the story
   when the game ends.
Friendships, *en passant,* don't offer moves
   to recapture them.

They are a disarray of conversations,
   unfinished stories, hesitations left
   for the next cup of coffee, cold beer,
   glass of wine.
Like wine they age with time,
   their memory takes on substance.
Handshakes, embraces, the kiss on the cheek,
   these leave impressions when they're gone,
   blank places on a calendar, dust
   on a chessboard.

Of all the things that take our friends away,
   we forgive only death,
   but not with ease.

What Is This Shining?

One soul
  or many
  or none at all

A single life
  or a string of lives

Or a gravity in us equal
  to the bending
  of our light

Charles R. Castle, Jr. was born in Portland, Maine, in 1951. With deep ancestral roots in colonial New England, he grew up in rural Connecticut and went to college in the Adirondack Mountains of upstate New York.

Early in the 1970's Charles spent two summers hitchhiking across North America, one trip to Alaska where he fought muskeg fire in British Columbia, and a second trip across the United States where he found a home in Eugene, Oregon. During a career in healthcare education and public affairs, he visited El Salvador with the Catholic Health Association to witness the conditions of rural healthcare after the country's civil war. Charles retired in 2009, and since then he has been involved in housing for the homeless. These experiences are reflected in his work.

As a young writer Charles was published in *Hanging Loose*. He began writing poetry again after the death of his parents in 2014. He has three books: *Living with Patriarchs, A Season's Second Coming,* and *A Good-night in America.* His poems are included in several anthologies.

Made in the USA
Lexington, KY
25 September 2019